THE
ARMIES OF INDIA

THE
ARMIES OF INDIA

PAINTED BY

MAJOR A. C. LOVETT
THE GLOUCESTERSHIRE REGIMENT

The Naval & Military Press Ltd

Published by

The Naval & Military Press Ltd
Unit 5 Riverside, Brambleside
Bellbrook Industrial Estate
Uckfield, East Sussex
TN22 1QQ England

Tel: +44 (0)1825 749494

www.naval-military-press.com
www.nmarchive.com

In reprinting in facsimile from the original, any imperfections are inevitably reproduced and the quality may fall short of modern type and cartographic standards.

LIST OF ILLUSTRATIONS

1. His Majesty the King-Emperor
2. Corps present at the Siege and Assault of Delhi, 1857
3. Governor-General's Bodyguard
4. Governor's Bodyguard, Madras
5. Governor's Bodyguard, Bombay
6. 1st Duke of York's Own Lancers and 3rd Skinner's Horse
7. British Officers of Indian Cavalry
8. 6th King Edward's Own Cavalry and 8th Cavalry
9. 10th Duke of Cambridge's Own Lancers
10. 11th King Edward's Own Lancers
11. 12th Cavalry
12. 14th Murray's Jat Lancers
13. 15th Lancers
14. 18th King George's Own Lancers
15. 19th Lancers
16. The former "Hyderabad Contingent" Cavalry
17. 25th Cavalry

THE ARMIES OF INDIA

18. 27th Light Cavalry and 26th King George's Own Light Cavalry
19. 31st Duke of Connaught's Own Lancers
20. 32nd Lancers, 33rd Queen's Own Light Cavalry, and 34th Prince Albert Victor's Own Poona Horse
21. 37th Lancers, 35th Scinde Horse, and 36th Jacob's Horse
22. 38th King George's Own Central India Horse
23. Queen's Own Corps of Guides
24. No. 31 Mountain Battery
25. 2nd Queen's Own Sappers and Miners
26. 3rd Sappers and Miners
27. 1st and 3rd Brahmans
28. Rajput Regiments
29. 5th Light Infantry and 6th Jat Light Infantry
30. Pioneer Regiments
31. 15th Ludhiana Sikhs
32. 19th Punjabis
33. 20th Duke of Cambridge's Own Infantry and 30th Punjabis
34. Punjab Regiments
35. 22nd Punjabis
36. 24th Punjabis
37. 26th Punjabis
38. Dogras
39. 33rd Punjabis
40. 35th Sikhs
41. 39th Garhwal Rifles
42. 40th Pathans

LIST OF ILLUSTRATIONS

43. 42nd Deoli Regiment
44. 43rd Erinpura Regiment, 44th Merwara Infantry, and 108th Infantry
45. 45th Rattray's Sikhs
46. 46th and 33rd Punjabis
47. Frontier Force
48. Frontier Force
49. Carnatic Infantry
50. 82nd Punjabis
51. The former "Hyderabad Contingent" Infantry
52. 101st Grenadiers and 102nd King Edward's Own Grenadiers
53. Mahratta Infantry
54. Rajputana Infantry
55. 124th Duchess of Connaught's Own Baluchistan Infantry
56. 125th Napier's Rifles
57. 127th Queen Mary's Own Baluch Light Infantry
58. 2nd King Edward's Own Gurkha Rifles
59. 4th Gurkha Rifles
60. 6th Gurkha Rifles
61. 9th Gurkha Rifles
62. Major-General H.H. Maharaja Sir Pratap Singh Bahadur, G.C.S.I., K.C.B.
63. Colonel H.H. Maharaja Sir Ganga Singh, Bahadur of Bikaner, G.C.I.E., K.C.S.I.
64. Alwar Lancers
65. Jodhpur Sardar Risala
66. Bikaner Ganga Risala

THE ARMIES OF INDIA

67. Mysore Transport Corps and Mysore Lancers
68. Bharatpur Infantry
69. Imperial Service Troops
70. The Khyber Rifles
71. Kurram Militia
72. Off to Pension

CORPS PRESENT AT THE SIEGE AND ASSAULT OF DELHI, 1857

10TH DUKE OF CAM-
9TH BRIDGE'S OWN
HODSON'S HORSE LANCERS
(Hodson's Horse)

57TH
WILDE'S RIFLES
(Frontier Force)

32ND SIKH PIONEERS

55TH
COKE'S RIFLES
(Frontier Force)

QUEEN'S OWN CORPS
OF GUIDES
(Lumsden's)

1ST
KING GEORGE'S
OWN SAPPERS
AND MINERS

22ND
SAM BROWNE'S
CAVALRY
(Frontier Force)

54TH SIKHS
(Frontier Force)

21ST PRINCE
ALBERT VICTOR'S
OWN CAVALRY
(Frontier Force)
(Daly's Horse)

3RD QUEEN
ALEXANDRA'S
OWN GURKHA
RIFLES

2ND KING
EDWARD'S OWN
GURKHA RIFLES
(The Sirmoor Rifles)

56TH PUNJABI
RIFLES
(Frontier Force)

127TH QUEEN
MARY'S OWN
BALUCH LIGHT
INFANTRY

GOVERNOR-GENERAL'S BODYGUARD

DAFFADAR
Sayyid of Shahpur (Musalman)

GOVERNOR'S BODYGUARD, MADRAS
Madrasi Musalman

GOVERNOR'S BODYGUARD, BOMBAY
Musalman Rajput

1st DUKE OF YORK'S OWN
LANCERS
(SKINNER'S HORSE)
Hindustani Musalman

3rd SKINNER'S HORSE
Musalman Rajput

BRITISH OFFICERS

| 5TH CAVALRY | 23RD CAVALRY (Frontier Force) | 17TH CAVALRY | 26TH KING GEORGE'S OWN LIGHT CAVALRY | 11TH KING EDWARD'S OWN LANCERS (Probyn's Horse) | 4TH CAVALRY Daffadar *Jat Sikh* | 16TH CAVALRY Jemadar *Jat* |

6TH KING EDWARD'S OWN CAVALRY
8TH CAVALRY
Jāts

10TH DUKE OF CAMBRIDGE'S OWN LANCERS
(HODSON'S HORSE)
"THE QUARTER GUARD"

| British Officer | Dogra | Punjabi Musalman | Sikh | Punjabi Musalman | Pathan |

11TH KING EDWARD'S OWN LANCERS
(PROBYN'S HORSE)

RISALDAR
Durrani (Afghan)

12TH CAVALRY

JEMADAR
Dogra

14TH MURRAY'S JAT LANCERS
RISALDAR-MAJOR

15TH LANCERS (CURETON'S MULTANIS)

Honorary Native Commandant
NAWAB SIR HAFIZ MUHAMMAD ABDULLAH KHAN, K.C.I.E.

18TH KING GEORGE'S OWN LANCERS

Honorary Lieutenant
Hon. MALIK UMAR HAYAT KHAN, C.I.E.
Tiwana of Shahpur

(*Punjabi Musalman*)

19TH LANCERS (FANE'S HORSE)
Punjabi Musalman

THE FORMER "HYDERABAD CONTINGENT" CAVALRY

30TH LANCERS (GORDON'S HORSE)
    Lance Daffadar
        Jāt

        20TH DECCAN HORSE
            Sikh

                29TH LANCERS (DECCAN HORSE)
                    Risaldar
                      Dekhani Musalman

25TH CAVALRY (FRONTIER FORCE)
BANGASH
(*Pathan*)

27TH LIGHT CAVALRY
BRITISH OFFICER

26TH KING GEORGE'S OWN
LIGHT CAVALRY
DAFFADAR
Madrasi Musalman of the Carnatic

31st DUKE OF CONNAUGHT'S OWN LANCERS

DAFFADAR

Dekhani Mahratta

32ND LANCERS

LANCE DAFFADAR
Musalman Rajput

33RD QUEEN'S OWN LIGHT CAVALRY

DAFFADAR
Kaimkhani

34TH PRINCE ALBERT VICTOR'S OWN POONA HORSE

Ratore Rajput

37TH LANCERS
(BALUCH HORSE)
Baluch

35TH SCINDE HORSE
KOT DAFFADAR
Baluch

36TH JACOB'S HORSE
Pathan
(All of the Derajat District)

38TH KING GEORGE'S OWN CENTRAL INDIA HORSE

LANCE DAFFADAR

Gakkar (Punjabi Musalman)

QUEEN'S OWN CORPS OF GUIDES (LUMSDEN'S)

INFANTRY   CAVALRY

Tanaoli (Pathan)   DAFFADAR

                        Adam Khel (Afridi)

No. 31 MOUNTAIN BATTERY
GUNNER
Punjabi Musalman

2ND QUEEN'S OWN SAPPERS AND MINERS

"THE WORKSHOPS"

HAVILDAR   SUBADAR
Christians

3RD SAPPERS AND MINERS

LANCE NAIK
Brahman of Oudh

JEMADAR
Dekhani Mahratti

1st AND 3rd BRAHMANS

SUBADAR
Brahmans of Oudh and North-West Provinces

RAJPUT REGIMENTS

7TH DUKE OF CONNAUGHT'S OWN RAJPUTS
Havildar

16TH RAJPUTS
(The Lucknow Regiment)
Subadar
Bhisti

8TH RAJPUTS

11TH RAJPUTS

2ND QUEEN'S OWN RAJPUT LIGHT INFANTRY

13TH RAJPUTS
(The Shekhawati Regiment)

5TH LIGHT INFANTRY   6TH JAT LIGHT INFANTRY
HAVILDARS
Musalman Rajput   *Jāt*

PIONEER REGIMENTS

128TH PIONEERS
Yusufzai (Pathan)

12TH PIONEERS
(The Kelat-i-Ghilzai Regiment)
Jat

34TH SIKH PIONEERS
Naik
Jat Sikh

81ST PIONEERS

64TH PIONEERS
Tamils

61ST KING GEORGE'S OWN PIONEERS
Madrasi Musalman

48TH PIONEERS
Labana Sikh

23RD SIKH PIONEERS
Jemadar

106TH HAZARA PIONEERS
Subadar-Major

34TH SIKH PIONEERS
Subadar-Major
Mazbi Sikhs

107TH PIONEERS
Kaimkhani (Musalman Rajput)

15TH LUDHIANA SIKHS
"THE COLOUR PARTY"
Jăt Sikhs

19th PUNJABIS

LANCE NAIK
Jat Sikh

BANGASH
(Pathan)

*Pathan of Upper
Swat Valley
(Out of Uniform)*

JEMADAR
Yusufzai (Pathan)

Punjabi Musalman

Afridi of Tirah

30TH PUNJABIS
AWAN
(*Punjabi Musalman*)

20TH DUKE OF CAMBRIDGE'S
OWN INFANTRY
(BROWNLOW'S PUNJABIS)
LANCE NAIK
Malikdin Khel (*Afridi*)

PUNJAB REGIMENTS

- 67TH PUNJABIS — Sepoy *Khatri Sikh*
- 29TH PUNJABIS — Subadar-Major *Punjabi Musalman*
- 24TH PUNJABIS — Subadar *Jāt Sikh*
- 21ST PUNJABIS — Subadar-Major *Adam Khel (Afridi)*
- 25TH PUNJABIS — Subadar-Major *Dogra*
- 28TH PUNJABIS — Subadar-Major *Jāt Sikh*
- 93RD BURMA INFANTRY — Subadar *Janjua (Punjabi Musalman)*
- 74TH PUNJABIS — Sepoy *Dogra*
- 76TH PUNJABIS — Subadar *Chach (Pathan)*
- 69TH PUNJABIS — Jemadar *Jāt Sikh*
- 87TH PUNJABIS — Havildar *Talap (Punjabi Musalman)*
- 84TH PUNJABIS — Sepoy *Tanaoli (Punjabi Musalman)*
- 72ND PUNJABIS — Sepoy *Punjabi Musalman*
- 91ST PUNJABIS (Light Infantry) — *Tanaoli (Punjabi Musalman)*

22ND PUNJABIS
Awan of Shahpur

24TH PUNJABIS

MALIKDIN KHEL   SUBADAR
(*Afridi*)   *Jāt Sikh*

26TH PUNJABIS
MALIKDIN KHEL
(*Afridi*)

DOGRAS

31ST PUNJABIS	37TH DOGRAS	27TH PUNJABIS	41ST DOGRAS	38TH DOGRAS
Havildar		Havildar		Subadar-Major

33RD PUNJABIS
SUBADAR
Punjabi Musalmans

35TH SIKHS

SUBADAR

39TH GARHWAL RIFLES
Garhwalis

40TH PATHANS

MALIKDIN KHEL
(*Afridi*)

42ND DEOLI REGIMENT

Honorary Major
H. H. Sir Umed Singh Bahadur, G.C.I.E., K.C.S.I.
Maharao of Kota (Rajputana)

43RD ERINPURA REGIMENT
COLOUR HAVILDAR
Mina

44TH MERWARA INFANTRY
HAVILDAR
Mer

108TH INFANTRY
KAIMKHANI
(*Rajputana Musalman*)

45TH RATTRAY'S SIKHS

"THE DRUMS"
Jăt Sikhs

46TH AND 33RD PUNJABIS
AFRIDIS
HAVILDAR

Zakka Khel *Malikdin Khel*
Oraksai *Kuki Khel* *Kambar Khel*

"FRONTIER FORCE"

51ST SIKHS
Piper
Punjabi Musalman

59TH SCINDE RIFLES
Gakkhar

56TH PUNJABI RIFLES
Sagri Khattaks

"FRONTIER FORCE"

57TH WILDE'S RIFLES	53RD SIKHS
Naik	Subadar
Adam Khel	*Sagri Khattak*
(Afridi)	

CARNATIC INFANTRY

63RD PALAMCOTTAH LIGHT INFANTRY
Tamil

83RD WALLAJAHBAD LIGHT INFANTRY
Christian

The 80th Honorary Colour with the Inscription, "Hyder Ally, Sholinghur, Hezira, 1195"

80TH CARNATIC INFANTRY

73RD CARNATIC INFANTRY

Subadars
Madrasi Musalmans

75TH CARNATIC INFANTRY
Christian

86TH CARNATIC INFANTRY
Madrasi Musalman

82ND PUNJABIS
AWAN
(*Punjabi Musalman*)

THE FORMER "HYDERABAD CONTINGENT" INFANTRY

98TH INFANTRY
Ahir of the Eastern Punjab

95TH RUSSELL'S INFANTRY
Hindustani Musalman

96TH BERAR INFANTRY
Jāt

94TH RUSSELL'S INFANTRY
Dekhani Musalman

97TH DECCAN INFANTRY
Rajput

102ND KING EDWARD'S OWN
GRENADIERS
Bagri Jāt

101ST GRENADIERS
. NAIK
Punjabi Musalman

MAHRATTA INFANTRY

110TH MAHRATTA LIGHT INFANTRY

116TH AND 114TH MAHRATTAS
Konkani Mahrattas

103RD MAHRATTA LIGHT INFANTRY
Subadar
Dekhani Mahrattas

RAJPUTANA INFANTRY

104TH WELLESLEY'S RIFLES
Subadar-Major
Gujar of Gujarat

112TH INFANTRY
Subadar
Sayyid Musalman

119TH INFANTRY
(The Multan Regiment)
Subadar
Gujar of Jaipur

123RD OUTRAM'S RIFLES
Lance Naik
Ratore Rajput

109TH INFANTRY
Khanazadah
Rajputana Musalman

113TH INFANTRY
Subadar-Major
Gujar of the Punjab

122ND RAJPUTANA INFANTRY
Rawat

124TH DUCHESS OF CONNAUGHT'S OWN BALUCHISTAN INFANTRY

"THE QUARTER GUARD"

LANCE NAIK
Khattak

Punjabi Musalman *Hazara*

125TH NAPIER'S RIFLES

SUBADAR-MAJOR
Jāt of Jaipur

HAVILDAR
Punjabi Musalmans

127TH QUEEN MARY'S OWN BALUCH
LIGHT INFANTRY

Brahni *Baluch from Dera Ghazi Khan* *Punjabi Musalman*

SUBADAR-MAJOR
Baluch of Khelat

2ND KING EDWARD'S OWN GURKHA RIFLES
(THE SIRMOOR RIFLES)

SUBADAR-MAJOR
Gurung Gurkha
King Edward's last Indian Orderly Officer

सु मे सन्तबीर जरू २/२ गोर्खा

4TH GURKHA RIFLES
Magar and Gurung Gurkhas
"A Rear-Guard Action"

6TH GURKHA RIFLES

9TH GURKHA RIFLES
A Khas Gurkha

टेकाबा ठाडा खत्री

Hon. Major-General
H.H. MAHARAJA SIR PRATAP SINGH BAHADUR
G.C.S.I., K.C.B.

Hon. Aide-de-Camp to His Majesty
Commandant Imperial Cadet Corps

Hon. Colonel
H.H. MAHARAJA SIR GANGA SINGH, BAHADUR OF BIKANER
G.C.I.E., K.C.S.I.
Hon. Aide-de-Camp to His Majesty
Commandant Bikaner Ganga Risala

ALWAR LANCERS

COMMANDANT
Chohan Rajput

JODHPUR SARDAR RISALA
Ratore Rajput

BIKANER GANGA RISALA
Ratore Rajput

MYSORE TRANSPORT CORPS 　　MYSORE LANCERS
Musalman　　　　　　　　　　*Madrasi Musalman*

BHARATPUR INFANTRY
THE COMMANDANT
Ját

IMPERIAL SERVICE TROOPS

Unit	Composition
PATIALA RAJINDRA LANCERS	Jāt Sikh
KASHMIR MOUNTAIN BATTERY	Dogra (Hindu)
KAPURTHALA INFANTRY	
JIND INFANTRY	} Jāt Sikhs
NABHA INFANTRY	
INDORE TRANSPORT CORPS	Commandant Dekhani Musalman
BAHAWALPUR MOUNTED RIFLES AND CAMEL TRANSPORT	
1ST KASHMIR INFANTRY	Commandant Dogra (Hindu)
SIRMOOR SAPPERS	Brahman
RAMPUR LANCERS	Rohilla
1ST HYDERABAD LANCERS	Mogul Musalman
2ND GWALIOR LANCERS	Mahratta
ALWAR INFANTRY	Shekhawati Musalman
BHARATPUR INFANTRY	Jāt
JAIPUR TRANSPORT CORPS	Commandant Rajput

THE KHYBER RIFLES
MALIKDIN KHEL

KURRAM MILITIA

SUBADAR
(Out of Uniform)
Turi

OFF TO PENSION
(A Sikh Officer)

www.ingramcontent.com/pod-product-compliance
Lightning Source LLC
Chambersburg PA
CBHW060927170426
43193CB00023B/2985